IN LEWY'S BODY

poems by

Vera Kewes Salter

Finishing Line Press
Georgetown, Kentucky

IN LEWY'S BODY

ACKNOWLEDGMENTS

Red Eft Review: "Absentee Ballot;" "Consistent with Lewy Body;" "Garbage;"
Medical Literary Messenger: "We Both Lose Words"
Right Hand Pointing: "Anosmia;" "Gone" (published as "Lost")
Persimmon Tree: "Things My Husband Told Me"
Writers Circle 2: "How to Measure Time"

Publisher: Leah Huete de Maines
Editor: Christen Kincaid
Cover Art: National Galleries of Scotland. Purchased 1949;
            Mabel Royds, *Dead Tulips*
Author Photo: Raya Salter
Cover Design: Elizabeth Maines McCleavy

Order online: www.finishinglinepress.com
            also available on amazon.com

Author inquiries and mail orders:
Finishing Line Press
PO Box 1626
Georgetown, Kentucky 40324
USA

Contents

Lewy Body Dementia (LBD) is a progressive disease associated with abnormal deposits of a protein in the brain. These deposits affect chemicals that can lead to problems with thinking, movement, behavior and hallucinations. The disease, often confused with Parkinson's, is diagnosed through clinical observation as there are no definitive biological markers available while a person is alive.

Absentee Ballot

Decades ago I moved in with him
in an excess of passion and never left.
I lived my own life though I may
have overindulged his whims.

Today as I bring him his ballot,
he asks for the Argonwald 1916
letter opener my mother
gave him for his 41st birthday.

I pace as he slowly slits
the envelope and pulls out
the ballot and the second
envelope with stiff fingers.

He reads the instructions
and asks whether he should
fill in the circles straight
across the top.

I give him a pen and watch
as he slowly colors the bubbles,
eases the ballot into the secure
envelope and signs on a slant.

I tell him that today's date
is written 10.10.2020. I drive
us to the post office. How much
is love and how much duty?

Garbage

He knows he must put it out on Thursday
but is not sure which day is Thursday.

He insists on making his own food, so I set a can
of Campbell's Chunky Chili Mac on the counter.

Orange and beige pills in little green boxes
labelled for each day are often skipped.

He wakes to see a pregnant feral cat break
into the house as he feels the weight of a baby

in his arms. He does eat the ham and cheese
sandwich I make, and we sit close together

on the bottom of the stairs and remember
the many homes where we once lived.

Consistent with Lewy Body

He sits with his hands in his lap
      unsure where he put them,
watches two women, one tall one short,
      walk through the closet door.

His swollen feet shuffle soggy paper towels
      to clean droplets from
the speckled tile floor -- he showers,
      I mop -- then towel water from his back.

At breakfast he asks:
      Why am I in Lewy's body?
we hang our answers
      on a clothesline,

read the paper and pray
      for a free and fair election—
together go into the garden,
      turn on the sprinkler,

admire the round red hibiscus
      he planted last year,
watch a tiger swallowtail
      drink nectar from a tiger lily.

At night he inspects the house,
      turns on the porch lights,
locks the terrace door
      that I left open.

Things My Husband Told Me

When college fell apart I returned
my burgundy Mustang and joined the Marines.

I was in my new uniform when a friend called
out to me in horror as I crossed a San Francisco street.

We marched through the City of Hue before
it was destroyed and returned through the rubble.

I loved hearing Dionne Warwick blasted
over loudspeakers by Hanoi Hannah.

I jumped out of my well-dug foxhole
when an armadillo jumped in.

I felt warm as a baby in the arms
of the corpsman who carried me out with malaria.

We loaded body bags from the *Forrestal* fire
onto our hospital ship; there were more dead than they said.

They did not want black leaders but had
no choice after so many soldiers were killed.

The commander sat on the hillside as my
squad led this large Tet Offensive operation.

I told the radio man to go to the back but he said
I'm coming for you and slumped dead over my body.

Airlifted to a field hospital under gunfire, I saw
a soldier strangle a wounded prisoner in his bed.

At home, I discarded my uniform and almost
joined the Weather Underground, but married instead.

Trigger

Newspaper lies on his lap,
black and white picture of
Marines resting in the dirt.

A tear rolls down the ridge of his
nose, as his face lengthens
into a distorted shape.

Vivid before him
the baby face of the soldier
he failed to protect.

Anosmia

We sleep side by side
　　　in the same firm bed
　　　　　　loyal to each other

for over forty years. I savor the scent
　　　of cologne on his chest.
　　　　　　He cannot smell

the Joy he gave me. I gag on the gas
　　　left un-lit on the stovetop.
　　　　　　He cannot smell

the bread burning in the oven.
　　　I enjoy the flavor of baked sole.
　　　　　　He remembers

how it used to taste. He grows
　　　fragrant roses and lilies
　　　　　　for me.

We walk by the pond admiring the ducks
　　　and cormorants. I imagine green
　　　　　　meadows and buttercups.

He sees a battlefield over the hill
　　　and tastes the smell
　　　　　　of gunpowder.

Gold Bands

The wedding ring slipped off
his thin finger.

After an anguished search
he found it caught on a deli-bag

in the refrigerator.
He rarely wears it now.

He commissioned our rings
from an artist on Walnut Street

forty-eight years ago. Twenty
years later, he arranged for small

diamonds to be fitted into the filigree
holes in the gold bands.

I help him find the jewelry box key
as he dresses for his neurology appointment.

He slips the ring on his finger.

Diagnosis

My husband was not labeled
with PTSD until fifty years
after he returned from Vietnam.

In 2017, his doctor sent my husband
to a neurologist to check for Parkinson's
because of his tremor and hallucinations.

The neurologist ruled out Parkinson's
and diagnosed his shuffling walk
as Extrapyramidal Disorder.

The VA did not deem Veterans exposed
to Agent Orange with Parkinson-like symptoms
eligible for disability until 2021.

In 2019 I did an internet search,
and found his multiple symptoms
on a Lewy Body checklist.

I asked the neurologist if my husband
had Lewy Body Disease. He added
Lewy Body Dementia to the chart.

Found*

Difficulty planning or keeping track of sequences
disorganized speech and conversation
episodes of confusion
poor sense of direction and spatial
relationships   forgetfulness
trouble with problem solving and multitasking
fluctuating levels of concentration

Rigidity and stiffness
shuffling walk
balance problems tremor
slowness of movement
weak voice
decrease in facial expression

Hallucinations - seeing or hearing things
that are not really present
depression apathy
delusions anxiety acting out dreams
falling out of bed
daytime sleepiness

Dizziness
lightheadedness
sensitivity to heat and cold
sexual dysfunction
urinary incontinence   poor sense of smell
constipation
transient   loss   of consciousness

*Comprehensive *LBD Symptom Checklist*
Lewy Body Dementia Association

Anger

you saw
the anger
in my eyes
apologized
though not
sure why
your chin
felt smooth
as we
embraced
maybe
you will eat
today

Surreal

He sees Captain Morgan stare through
the window in his red brocade jacket
      with a bandana over his flowing hair.

The policeman who answers his
emergency call circles the house
      but does not find an intruder.

Nine black squirrels jump through
the bedroom window screen
      and disappear up the chimney.

He drags logs to the fireplace
and lights the flames to smoke
      the squirrels out.

At night he cleans the ash
from the grate and turns
      on the porch lights.

Things My Husband Tells Me Now

Help me stop the baby in the blue onesie
from reaching the fireplace flames.

It's disgusting how hard it is
to get my puny arms into my t-shirt.

There is a dead hobby horse
on the glass table outside.

My brain is a scattered handful
of cotton seeds.

Do you see the man climbing
the electric pole?

Are you sure the spider
on the floor is real?

The Bird Feeder

The black squirrel hangs upside down
and eats seeds from the squirrel-proof bird feeder.

It was in the basement where my husband left it. He fed
wild birds every winter and hung red hot suet.

I did not stand and watch nuthatches and cardinals,
didn't question his constant trips to Home Depot

where he bought dozens of tubes of caulk
which now line up on a shelf unused and dry.

Today I meddle in tasks with his advice. I've learned
how to charge a cordless drill and drive a screw.

And as the snow falls, we find a way to feed the birds.

We Both Lose Words

I push something square
into a silver machine

and eat it for breakfast. White
emptiness where the words should be.

He supplies the word *toaster*.
I kneel to tighten his shoes.

As we walk around the park
we struggle to find the word

for a water bird with a snake-like neck
that dips its head below the surface.

We see a lone sailboat moored near
the winter shore,

watch gulls crack clams and mussels
on the asphalt pier.

Then, in sudden unison shout—
cormorant.

Winter Afternoon

Angles of sunlight cover
    us as we lie on our bed
        on this false spring day.

He remembers every singer
    and word of each song as
        the American Songbook plays.

His fingers are weak
    contorted. He regrets that
        thoughts are hard to form.

Nerve pain down my leg,
    music in the background,
        we rest in the place that is home.

Red Tulips

I bought them on a gloomy February
afternoon overwrapped in brown
paper—one dozen closed oval heads.

They stood tall, narrow, acute,
their stems visible
through the rounded glass vase.

The next two mornings their scarlet
petals amazed me—orange and black
centers open toward the sun.

Now a dozen stems topped with black
stamen and yellow pistils.
Burnished ochre leaves scatter
misshapen on the table.

How to Measure Time

On this date I have lived one month longer than my mother

The earth is 4.54 billion years old

My sister was pushed into a long white crypt after eighty-three years

The Long Now Clock ticks once a year
and the cuckoo comes out on the millennium

Mouthless moth larvae feed on wallaby grass for two years
and metamorphose to seek sex and starve in four days

Seventeen-year cicadas emerge on time for their few weeks of life

My husband made coffee at 6.40 in the evening because he thought it
was morning

A Normal Morning

He sits at the bottom of the steps
    and struggles on his socks.

I bring his coffee
    to the table.

He recalls the line
    I never saw the sea.

I look up the poem
    and read it out loud.

He supplies the word *gorgon*
    to fit in my crossword puzzle.

Together we search for the spider
    that is not on the curtain.

Ambiguous Loss

I view us in the mirror as I hold
you steady to brush your teeth.
Feel your rich brown skin
as I lift your legs to the bed.
Find comfort as I lie warm next to you—
rest in the space between your breaths.
Hope that the two small pills I feed
you will allow twelve hours of sleep.

I rise early alone. Branches tap
the window. I watch the dark sky
turn pale then bright blue. Magenta
maple leaves cover the driveway
and coat the forked tree. A single red
leaf rests on the juniper bush.

Gone

The months are going backwards.
Time is cut in half.

It is June and it should
be getting colder.

I saw a firefly last night.
A Rose of Sharon bloomed.

The hollyhock lies
on the ground.

Words become a little clearer
move back to silence.

Explosions go off
inside his eyelids.

There is a hammer holding
the door shut.

Vera Kewes Salter is a care partner for her husband of fifty years who has a diagnosis of Lewy Body Dementia. He is a United States Marine Corps veteran who served in Vietnam. They live in New Rochelle, New York.

Vera was born and raised in London, England, in a family of refugees from Europe. In 1969 she moved to the United States and married into an African American family, had two children and earned her doctorate in sociology. These varied perspectives are integral to her work.

She is a lifelong activist and has worked professionally as a healthcare planner. Her work has appeared in *Red Eft Review, Nixes Mate Review, Prometheus Dreaming, Medical Literary Messenger, Judaica Mismor Anthology, Right Hand Pointing, Persimmon Tree, Writing in a Woman's Voice* and other publications.